Becoming a Londoner
Our Creative Campaign!

Published by:
The Barbara Melunsky Refugee Youth Agency Ltd,
(known as **REFUGEEYOUTH**)
2009
ISBN: 978-0-9563626-0-5
www.refugeeyouth.org
info@refugeeyouth.org.uk
020 7793 7156
Registered Charity no: 1094296
Company Registered in England and Wales no: 4343703

RefugeeYouth is a growing and active community of young people from different refugee communities working together across London. We work and learn together by researching the issues that affect our lives, formulating and experimenting with solutions to our own problems.

Becoming a Londoner

Our Creative Campaign!

By RefugeeYouth

London...

Stangers coming, strangers leaving
Strangers knowing nothing but what they're seeing
Eye contact is completely against the rules.

Don't touch, don't speak
Keep looking mild, looking meek
Hold tightly to your bag.

Keep your smile in check, newspaper up
Prepare to get off at the correct stop
Inch away from the pierced, the tattooed, the dyed, the
dirty, the loud, the bold, the colourful, the different.

Refugee Youth...

Chosen carefully, haphazardly, randomly, laughingly.
A hello, a handshake, a smile, a seat.
Forget names, forget information, forget dinner – someone's
just made it. But wash your own plate!
A jam session, a dance session
Lose self-consciousness, Find self-confidence
Lose your inhibitions, Fine your Self.
Tea?
A laugh, a kiss, a hug, a walk together, a goodbye –
See you tomorrow!
A family of friends found and you didn't even know
you were looking for it.

Contents

Section

Section

Section

Introduction

Our Creative Campaign!

This book has been written collectively by young people in RefugeeYouth. It is one of the results of a long-term, ongoing project which we call our 'Creative Campaign'. In these pages we reflect on the context of our lives, our experiences of the services that exist to support us, and our own solutions to the problems we face.

Through our Creative Campaign, we hope to make change on 3 levels:

Through coming together and exploring our own lives, we learn about how to make change ourselves. In RefugeeYouth young people inspire and support each other to lead their own projects, youth groups and activities to improve their own lives and those of their peers. We invite any young people who want to do the same to come and join us!

Through working with practitioners and reflecting back to them the way the services they provide are experienced, we hope to inspire and motivate them. We hope that they will learn with us about how to inform their practice based on knowledge and learning from young people.

We hope to contribute to the wider dialogue surrounding refuge and immigration; to challenge negative public and media opinions. We hope to strengthen the campaign for a just and fair asylum system that recognises refugees as human beings, valuing and upholding their human rights.

Participatory Action Research

In RefugeeYouth, our work is based on the principles of Participatory Action Research[1], and 'Becoming a Londoner' is an example of this. Through Participatory Action Research, people come together to explore the issues that affect their lives, realise the knowledge that they have from their ownexperiences, and work collectively to formulate solutions to their own problems.

Unlike traditional research, Participatory Action Research is 'insider' research, conducted by and for the people it directly affects, and is primarily concerned with producing change rather than reports. This book is only one part of an ongoing cycle of action, reflection, learning, planning and further action in which young people in RefugeeYouth are engaged.

1 For an accessible introduction to Participatory Action Research read
Stringer, E (1999) Action Research, Sage

How did this book come about?

In 2006 we were approached by the Greater London Authority to work with them on the Mayor's Refugee Integration Strategy for London. We agreed, and a team of young people in RefugeeYouth set about researching their own lives and experiences and those of their peers, by designing and running a series of creative workshops and focus groups. Over 3 months a total of 92 young people living in 20 different London boroughs, aged 12 – 25, originating from 20 different countries were involved. We made a creative presentation of our findings to the Board for Refugee Integration, London.

However, consultation can be very depressing, and the young people who got involved along the way wanted action! We urged the Mayor to keep working with us, and set about designing a week long residential workshop, to which we invited young people from across our network to work together to investigate in greater depth the issues raised in the early workshops and explore solutions.

Introduction • Participatory Action Research

We used drama, dance, music, drumming, singing and film-making to explore our lives and create powerful pieces to demonstrate solutions around the issues of education, housing, social services, social life and safety.

Back in London, in July 2007, RefugeeYouth took over City Hall for a day bringing together 115 young people and more than 50 policy makers and service providers to share our findings and start working together to find solutions. Through a whole day of workshops, we explored the issues using drumming, dancing, singing, placard making, mask making, t-shirt printing and henna painting (all the activities led by young people).

We created a dramatic, musical demonstration that proceeded down the ramp from the top to the bottom of City Hall. Intensive discussions with the guests followed after which guests were invited to make a written pledge to follow-up after the event. The day ended with performances staged in the Scoop Arena outside City Hall. Members of RefugeeYouth including a Somali dance group, a Congolese band, Albanian traditional dancers, street dancers and rappers and salsa dancers entertained and energised not just the guests, the young people, and the City Hall workers but passing members of the public too.

Since then, the project hasn't stopped; young people in RefugeeYouth continue to develop and lead exciting and innovative youth projects and we're on a constant outreach mission to involve as many young people as possible.

New knowledge and learning is also generated though
our advocacy work. We have designed and run creative
workshops and presentations for Social Workers, housing
providers, Youth Work students, University staff and
lecturers, and the Regional Director of the Home Office.
Typically, a team of young people comes together to explore
their own experiences in relation to the matter in hand.
Together they design and facilitate a workshop through which
they creatively convey their messages (using role play, games,
art, invisible theatre etc) and explore with others the issues
raised and possible solutions. The process can be painful, but
we also feel powerful when we realise that the learning from
our own experiences can help to change practice and policy.
Every time we do a piece of work like this, we learn more,
and more young people become involved.

This year we are pleased to have secured funding from the
Barrow Cadbury Trust to publish Becoming a Londoner.
We worked to involve all the new young people who have
become involved in RefugeeYouth since the project began.
Through a residential weekend and a series of focus groups
and creative workshops we have revisited the issues raised,
and through a collective process of editing and design we
have pulled together some of what we have learnt as a
community of young people working together in RefugeeYouth
over the last 6 years.

All of the quotations are
taken directly from young
people who have been
involved in various stages
of the process. The case
studies are the true sto-
ries of individuals, though
some names have been
changed.

Introduction • How did this book come about?

What do we hope to achieve with this book?

With this book we, young people from RefugeeYouth, hope to inspire!

We hope to inspire young people to get active in their communities. We hope to inspire policy-makers, professionals and funders to support young refugees to take a lead in their communities, so that we can change our own lives and those of our peers, and become active young Londoners.

Focusing on the problems we face can leave us feeling helpless and hopeless. We do not want to simply moan and then feel disappointed when nothing changes. Instead we want to demonstrate and celebrate all the positive things that we young people are already doing within our communities and amongst our peers, which make real, significant, positive and immediate change to our lives in London.

We want to share our learning with you because we believe that by working and learning together we can make change, so that young people who come here to seek refuge in years to come don't have to suffer some of the things that we have suffered. We also want to share the good things; so that young people can benefit and gain from the support and services and experiences that we know work well.

Much of what we write can be applied not just in London, but across the UK. We write about London life because it is what we know and where we are starting from, but we would love to build networks and dialogue with young people, service providers and policy makers across the UK.

For us, the process of writing this book has been amazing. It has brought us together as a community, and taught us a lot about ourselves and each other. However, for us, the book itself is not as important as what we do with the knowledge and learning collected within it. We are concerned with ACTION!
We want to use our learning to work together with people who impact on the lives of young refugees across the UK, to explore, reflect and learn together in order to make change where we can.

So read on, and then get in touch so we can start working together...!

What is RefugeeYouth?

RefugeeYouth is a growing and active community of young people from different refugee communities working together across London.

Our Mission:

RefugeeYouth is dedicated to breaking down isolation and combating alienation and despair amongst young refugees by supporting opportunities for their development. We aim to create an environment of friendship and belonging in which young refugees gain strength and power, collectively and as individuals, through creative learning

RefugeeYouth was set up with the aim of becoming an organisation *of* young people, rather than a service *for* young people. With this in mind, we develop as a resourced network; a place where young people can come and test out their ideas, and get the support and resources they need in order to work together to make positive change. We work and learn together by researching the issues that affect our lives, formulating and experimenting with solutions to our own problems.

In RefugeeYouth, a whole range of young people, aged 14-30, from different backgrounds come together, and so this document is a reflection of many different experiences. At the last count we were more than 400 people representing 36 different countries. Some of us came here alone, some with our families, some of us were born here to refugee parents. Some of us have refugee status, many of us are still waiting for a decision, some of us have been refused refugee status but are stuck, unable to return home. We also welcome into RefugeeYouth young people who are not refugees. We welcome anyone who wants to stand under the banner of RefugeeYouth because we have learned that life is richer when we work together.

Our programme of work has developed into 3 interdependent levels: **fun, food and friendship, leadership Development,** and **Action to Bring About Change.**

fun, food and friendship

is the basis of everything we do. In RefugeeYouth we aim to create a space where young refugees can find belonging. We build relationships, share and explore culture and start to feel at home through cooking and eating together, exploring London and creative arts work. Our weekly youth groups are a platform for new young people to get involved in RefugeeYouth, and are aimed at involving those who are most isolated and most vulnerable. Our regular 'Mix It Up' events (big all-day youth-led arts festivals) - bring together young people from across our network in celebration. We don't offer any formal advice or guidance services, but we 'walk the path' with people, supporting individuals to deal with all the issues that arise in their lives, whether that's helping someone to fill in a form or write a letter, accompanying them to a scary court case, or listening when they need to talk. Through all of our many and varied experiences we have a lot to offer each other.

Youth leadership

is at the heart of all our work. In RefugeeYouth, young people are supported to lead and develop all the projects and activities, and to learn the skills they need to go out and work in their own communities. This happens through formal training, informal support and mentoring, and through creating the conditions where young people can take risks and test out their ideas. With plenty of reflection and rigorous evaluation we learn from everything we do together.

Action to Bring About Change

is the name that we give to the advocacy side of our work. It's about learning from what we do together, as well as the experiences of our own lives, and using that learning to make change; amongst ourselves, with the professionals who impact on the lives of young refugees, and with the wider public.

* World Remix, Women'sWorth and Mustaqbal are currently our weekly youth groups. Refuge In Films is our annual Film Festival.

Becoming a Londoner
Our Creative Campaign!

The Context of our Lives explores some of the many issues that affect young refugees' lives

Our Experiences of Services explores young refugees' experiences, both good and bad, with The Home Office, Education, Social Services, Employment, Housing, Health, Safety & Crime and Youth Services

Finding our own Solutions explores what we as young people have learnt about good youth work through working together, how important our positive experiences of good youth work have been, and what support we need to do the work ourselves

The Context of Our Lives

What is important to remember is that when we come here as children, whether alone or with our families, it is never our choice. We are here because someone decided it was what was best for us. When we get here we have to justify and defend the decisions made for us by adults and we feel we often get punished for them.

At the same time, young people who come to the UK to start a new life show courage and resilience. We have so much to offer and share with the rest of the community but sometimes the context of our lives makes it difficult.

Asylum Policy and the three 'D's

Current asylum policy can have devastating effects on our lives, particularly for young people who come to the UK alone, unac-companied by family. Many young people are living in limbo for years, waiting for decisions on cases.This time is characterised by uncertainty and fear:

*"You can't speak to the police,
can't access health care, can't access rights.
You can't be a Londoner, because you're trying to be invisible"*

Very few young people get refugee status before turning 18, and so for many of us, the prospect of turning 18 is full of fear rather than excitement. Quite simply, some of us in this country are scared to grow up. The 3 'D's – Dispersal, Detention and Deportation, are all frightening prospects:

"When I had a refusal I had to sign in every week
[with the Home Office] and every time
I thought they might detain me.
I used to pack my bag with all my precious belongings just in case
they deported me"

"When I was 19 they dispersed me, sending me from Lewisham
where I had all my friends and contacts since I was 15 years old,
and was studying hard at College, to Birmingham, where
I know no-one and now have nothing to do"

"I will feel like a Londoner when I get papers.
I can study, work, and have no fear to go anywhere"

The Stigma of being a Refugee

"As soon as they find out I'm a refugee I'm dead in the class"

This is often the excuse for much of the bullying that
we experience:

"In my class, one guy tries to bully me saying,
'the Home Office is coming!' "

Much of the rhetoric used by certain branches of the media
and certain politicians alienates and criminalises refugees
and asylum seekers. As a result, most people don't even
know what a refugee is!

"When people understand the issues that make people refugees
they won't hate us anymore.
We came here for refuge.
We want to stay here and survive,
we have no other hope except staying here"

What is a Refugee ?

The 1951 United Nations Convention Relating to
the Status of Refugees defines a refugee as a person who:
"owing to a well founded fear of being persecuted for
reasons of race, religion, nationality, membership
of a particular social group, or political opinion, is outside
the country of his or her nationality, and is unable to,
or owing to such fear is unwilling to avail him/herself
of the protection of that country."

Our definition of Refugee

The RefugeeYouth definition of young refugees includes
young people between the ages of 14 and 30 years,
from 5 continents and speaking many different languages.
It includes young people who have been in this country
for a few months, a few years, or who were born here as
children of refugees. It includes those who arrived as
unaccompanied children, and those who came with their
families. It includes young people living in ordinary homes
with parents, with other family members, with friends from
their own or other communities, or alone. It includes those
living in hostels, 'looked after' in children's homes or by
foster parents, living in reception or detention centres.
It includes those who are homeless. It includes those
whose permanent or temporary residence in the UK has
been approved, those whose application for asylum is
currently being considered, and those whose application
has been refused but are unable to return home.

The Context of Our lives

Family Pressures

There can be considerable pressure on young people who are here in the UK with their families. Parents worry about their children here, they want us to keep hold of their culture. Parents often put pressure on us to bring money into the household, as well as to achieve academically.

"Mum is my only support, but she blocks me.
She is blind to what I do. If you don't bring money into the home they think you are just wasting time"

Young people often end up taking on many adult responsibilities within their families and communities:

"We end up becoming translators,
legal advisors, housing advisors
and carers for the whole community"

As a result many of us lose the opportunity to live out our childhoods. All young people in every community make change by challenging their elders, but this is harder if parents are lonely and dependent on their children. Parents are often stressed, depressed and isolated, and this in turn damages family relationships:

"Parents don't get to experience this culture like we do.
I don't know anywhere I can take my mum where
she can explore things like I can in my youth group.
Parents need escapism and new experiences too"

London life

London life can be full of excitement and opportunity but it can also be scary and lonely:

"Being a Londoner can make you very big and can also make you very small"

We will travel long distances to be with people with whom we feel comfortable; those who share our language, culture or interests. However, London is a big city and traveling around it is really expensive. Access to affordable transport is really important for us. Having access to good transport also helps us to feel safe in London:

"If you have a bus pass you're ok"

"You have to travel around to find a place where you feel comfortable"

Often we can only engage in projects and activities if we can get our travel expenses covered. London can be scary if you don't have strong support networks and local knowledge:

"I feel like I'm living in an angry generation. Sometimes I want to mix with people around me and experience being a Londoner, and I find that they don't want to mix with me"

But London can also be an amazing place, where we are free to be ourselves. All of the young people we spoke to relish the opportunity to be part of London life and many of them simply crave the security that comes from having permission to stay here, so that they can get on with being a Londoner.

"What does it take to become a Londoner? Chicken 'n' chips of course!"

The Content of Our lives

Some of the key issues for young refugees

Losing our childhood

If we come to the UK alone....
- we have to deal with everything ourselves; lawyers, Home Office papers, court rooms, legal jargon
- we can feel lonely and depressed without support, advice or guidance

If we come to the UK with family.....
- we often have to take responsibility for our whole family
- it's left to us to translate, interpret and figure out how the system works
- family roles become confused and family and community relations can break down

Leading a double life

- there is conflict between generations; our parents want to preserve their culture and protect their children
- we are trying to live in two cultures
- The result is that we end up not fitting in anywhere: we are trying to grow up and figure out who we are in amongst all this

18th birthday

- we are frightened to grow up because everything changes
- we are in danger of losing our status, benefits, education and housing
- we fear the '3 Ds' – Dispersal, Detention, Deportation
- we are suddenly considered adults and support is taken away from us

Age dispute

- many of us have our age disputed, either by the Home Office or Social Services or both
- the process of age assessment is inhumane and degrading
- those of us here alone whose age is disputed get no support from social services

Criminalisation

- refugees are portrayed as criminals by many sections of the media and many politicians
- prejudice and discrimination towards refugees has become legitimised as a mainstream viewpoint
- the asylum system criminalises people, promoting a culture of disbelief and treating refugees as guilty until proven innocent

Networks

- we don't have the family, community and friendship networks that people who were born here have
- we don't know the systems here, and neither do our families

Living in limbo

- many of us are living in uncertainty waiting for the Home Office to make a decision – sometimes for years
- with no papers many of us are unable to travel, work or study
- it's impossible to plan for the future. We have no control over our own lives
- we are always waiting for someone else to make a decision
- sometimes we feel totally powerless; like we don't exist
- we become dependent on limited benefits, when we have the ambition and the skills to work
- we are not able to follow our dreams or gain qualifications or employment experience
- sometimes we are forced into illegal work or criminal activity in order to survive

Our experiences of services

The Home Office

Many of us have had some really difficult experiences with the Home Office. We sometimes feel that we are treated like criminals. The whole process of applying for asylum is terrifying. We have to tell our stories over and over again and we are usually treated with suspicion.

"It's like we are guilty until proven innocent – they make you feel like a liar"

Many young people have their age disputed. This is a totally humiliating experience. Even if Social Services recognises a young person to be under 18, the Home Office can still dispute this. Whilst your age is disputed you are not given any leave to remain.

"My age was disputed by the Home Office. In my second interview the Home Office interviewer realised she had got it wrong, and that I really was only 16, but she told me she was unable to change it because her manager had already approved what she had said in the first place"

"It says 'age disputed' on my ID card, which is my only proof of identity"

Being interviewed and going to court is really scary, especially if we are on our own. The people are rude and interviews can go on for hours at a time with no break. They ask so many questions, some of which seem totally irrelevant. We often feel accused and blamed, and usually we don't know our rights enough to stand up for ourselves.

"The Home Office is totally against you. The interviewers try and scare you and you get nervous and confused"

"They ask the same question 3 times in slightly different ways, to try and make you say different things"

Sometimes translators get it wrong, and different translators can interpret your words differently.

"I had 3 interviews with different translators...
and then they said my story is inconsistent"

The legal jargon that is used by the Home Office is really hard for us to understand, and often we are left on our own trying to understand what they are saying.

Muna's Story

I came to UK from Somalia alone and aged 15 and I went to live with some distant family in London. Last year I had some real family problems, and it became so difficult that I couldn't live with them anymore. I went to Migrant Help Line for support, and because I am now 19 they sent me to NASS (National Asylum Support Service). NASS could only house me outside of London, even though I was enrolled in college in Lewisham and that is where all my friends are and where my whole life was based. They could not tell me where they would send me – but they told me I would have to go to Ashford until they found a place for me somewhere else.

In the meantime, they put me in a temporary hostel in Croydon. It was really horrible and I felt very lonely there. After 2 weeks they said they were coming to pick me up to take me to Ashford. I packed my bags and waited. It was Ramadan so I was tired and hungry. It got to 4 o'clock in the afternoon and no one came. I rang them and they said someone would be there before 11pm. I waited some more. They still didn't come. I unpacked my bags and went to bed. The next day, the same thing happened, and the next day. They left me waiting for 3 days in that hostel and no one told me what was happening. Each day they said they were coming, and no one turned up.

Finally they moved me to Ashford for 2 weeks, then to Birmingham, which is where I am now. The problems haven't ended though, because I have lost one whole academic year. There were no college spaces for me here, so now I am just waiting for September to come round again so I can get on with my studies and my life.

Education

Young refugees have a range of educational needs when we arrive in the UK. Our experiences range across a whole spectrum. Some us have received a high level of education, whilst others come from places where we never had access to education at all.

Young refugees face a host of educational problems when we come to London. If you don't speak English, you need to learn the language - and quickly:

"I remember the first day of school crying because I didn't know how to say I wanted to use the toilet"

For those who already speak English it is very frustrating to find yourself stuck in ESOL courses:

"I never needed an interpreter, so why did they put me in ESOL? They told me I had to do ESOL, so I did it because I didn't want to stay at home"

It is challenging to understand the mainstream educational system because it is very different from what we are used to.

"The system was very different from my own country. I never had anyone to explain how the system works"

It is also extremely difficult to find a place at a school and to fit in when you get here.

"I had to commute to Richmond for college each morning, because that was the only college place available. I had to wake up early and do extra work to have the same quality of work as others, because of the language"

"I used to say I was a refugee from Guinea but I felt like no one wanted to be my friend. In Richmond, people are very white. I had to get into it and act a certain way to fit in. You adapt and get used to it"

Our experiences of services • Education

Some teachers have very low expectations of us when English is not our first language. Low expectations can make us frustrated and disruptive and sometimes we give up on our education.

"They always say " don't worry, you're doing good." They never say "you could do better' – they never push us"

Extra support can be necessary, but it can also be stigmatising; young people who get one to one support stand out in the classroom.

"What works is when they have a young person, not an old person who is more like a parent, but a mentor; it becomes a group thing, supporting each other. It's a natural, nicer way"

Our parents have very high expectations of us, but they don't understand the systems so they can't support us through the education system. We don't know what options are available and we feel we often get bad careers advice. We often end up choosing the wrong course. So many talented artists or future teachers or social workers are studying in the wrong field. For example, many of us who study travel and tourism don't even have a passport to travel!

"I loved acting and wanted to study expressive arts – but there was no way my parents would let me. They couldn't see how I could make a living at it – there's no arts industry in Somalia. So I did a degree in Business Studies and hated it"

Those of us who are here on our own lack guidance and support. With an uncertain decision from the Home Office we sometimes wonder what the point of studying is.

"If you're here on your own you don't know what to do; there is no one to advise you or encourage you"

"It was my youth worker who pushed me to start studying. I thought, 'what's the point? They're gonna deport me anyway'. She said 'so if they do you'll have something to take with you' "

At College we suffer financial hardship. Without leave to remain, we are not entitled to Education Maintenance Allowance. When we reach 19 we move from Income Support to Job Seekers' Allowance, and are no longer allowed to study full time. So many of us have to choose between finishing our A Levels and losing all our benefits, or dropping out of education all together.

Accessing Higher Education can be very difficult. If you haven't been in the UK for 3 years you can't access student loans and hardship funds. When our immigration status is uncertain, Universities will often charge us overseas fees.

"It's a shame that I was being restricted from going to university just because I haven't been in the country for more than three years. Being a refugee means that my life is here now; I have no choice, I need to move forward. Education is my only option".

Even with a student loan, the decision to go to university involves a big risk:

"Should I give up Job Seekers' Allowance and Housing Benefit?
Will I find enough paid work to pay for everything?
Will I be able to work and still attend lectures?
Who can I fall back on if it all goes wrong?"

Young refugees have added burdens. We need money not only to support ourselves but to support our families here (which is of course a role reversal – the children are often the breadwinners in refugee families) and often we need some left over to support our families back home.

"I always wanted to achieve...it was a challenge but when I saw what other people were doing it gave me a passion and I'm really proud of what I'm doing. What almost put me off in education was supporting my family. It's a very traditional thing that young people support their family. It was a bad time and I did leave the course for a month. That was the lowest for me. A lot of people go through that."

Our experiences of services • Education

Young refugees' perspectives on good practice in schools and colleges

Do

- Point us in the direction of the support we need at home and at school
- Give us options – we want to achieve and succeed
- Provide assistants in the classroom who can support us and help us to catch up
- Find us mentors who understand what we are going through and who can be positive role models for us
- Be prepared to learn with us, and realise that you don't know everything

Don't

- Assume that we get support and guidance from home – either we're on our own or we are looking after our parents a lot of the time
- Assume that because we enter the school system late we are never going to achieve anything
- Ignore us if we are quiet
- Make it so we have to misbehave in order to get attention
- Send us away if we don't understand the culture of your classroom

Sara's Story

I was 16 when I came. I didn't say I was a refugee, I was just a normal student. I had to do some exams. They said to me, "Okay, what we realise from your grades is that you've done really well. Some people who have been here longer don't do so well." They said they accepted me as a quick learner and that they expected me to learn English over the summer. They were very kind. My sister was 17 when she came and she had to do ESOL. She's still doing ESOL. She wasn't given the chance to do what I did. I didn't get great grades, but they realised I was a hard worker. Now I'm doing Health and Social Care. They gave me a chance to really do what I want. If people give you a chance, you really get to learn. You can learn English every day. My college, through student services, supports me financially. They talk to me like I'm family and try their best to give me the proper support that I need. At Christmas they always remember me, they send me cards and stuff. Sometimes they give me special aid money over the holidays. They support me as myself, they know my religion and they are always attentive. They meet with me once a week to make sure that I'm doing well with my studies. If I'm having trouble, they take the time to work out a schedule with me, go over my goals and the things I need to do. If I have to meet with my solicitor when I have class, they tell me to go to class and they will contact my solicitor. At the end of the day, they have information that helps me. They always remember appointments and anything I need. They are always in touch.

Before we make any decisions, they always help me to get the relevant information. They want me to do well, stay in college and achieve my goals. That makes me feel strong. They give me a feeling of security and control. My academic and personal life is balanced; I'm not sacrificing anything. They treat everyone equally and fair. They are there for me and that makes life easier. From that, I learn to respect people in order to get what I need. I am really proud to know them because they strengthen my own pride and self-confidence.

Social Services

Between us we have a whole range of different experiences with Social Services. We have often found that young people living in different London boroughs receive different levels of support, especially financial support, and that feels very unfair.

"Social Workers all do it their own way – there are no rules"

It's hard to express how you feel, or put in a complaint, because you are very dependent on your Social Worker as a young person. Many of us do not even know what standard and level of support we should expect.

When you are here on your own without any family it is so important to have a good relationship with your Social Worker; sometimes they are all you've got.

"My Social Worker took me to the GP, opticians, picked me up from my home and called me regularly to see if I'm ok"

"My Social Worker was like a Mum to me; she understood and made me feel like she was thinking about me"

Good Social Workers will support you to get what you deserve:

"My Social Worker fights for my rights, standing by me like a Social Worker should"

"My Social Worker goes that extra mile, she admits that she is also learning, and she looks into stuff properly if she is not sure. She tries hard to find out what is going to work best for me"

On the other hand, we have had some difficult experiences and relationships with Social Workers. When we are assigned different Social Workers all the time it is very frustrating and disruptive; we have to start all over again. Sometimes we don't feel like we are getting the right support form our Social Workers:

"They don't want you to make your own choices. I love Maths and I wanted to do my A Level in Maths but my Social Worker recommended that I focus on ESOL instead. I did not feel encouraged to go for my dreams"

"Social Workers should help you learn how the system works, but not tell you what you can and can't do. Many times I found that my Social Worker was not passing on information to me about my rights and entitlements"

"Whenever I asked for something, my Social Worker would make me feel guilty and ungrateful. When I complained about my hostel being noisy and full of rats, he said I should be grateful I even have somewhere to live"

Many young people have their age disputed by Social Services; sometimes even when their age has been accepted by the Home Office. This is very confusing for us; we feel that Social Services are supposed to be on the side of young people and when they question us and accuse us of lying we don't know where to turn.

"It can feel like Social Services dispute someone's age because they don't have enough money in their budget to support another young person"

Many of us feel that we are given little long term guidance or warnings about the future and the changes we are likely to face with regard to our immigration status and our support services when we turn 18. Some of us feel that we are given bad advice and that the system is uncaring towards us.

"You're only 16 once, so if they waste your time you can't get it back"

Our experiences of services • Social Services

Perspectives on good practice for Social Workers

Do

- Tell us what we're entitled to and our rights

- Walk the path with us so that we can learn how to do things for ourselves

- Warn us about the future, and about what will happen when we turn 18

- Give us the support and guidance that we need in order to prepare us to cope with the responsibilities and problems to come

- Try and give us some geographical stability so that we can get on and build our lives

- Develop events and forums where we can learn about the services and structures that are there for us

- Develop *real* relationships with us and talk to us like *real* people

- Speak up on our behalf, and fight to try and get the best for us

- Link us up, introduce us to people, places and services

- Help us to stay on our case – we get so worried we can lose the plot

- Try and be consistent – it doesn't work if we have to see a different worker every week

- Think about how you interpret policy, and try and do this in line with other practitioners and services

Don't

- Hide our entitlements from us

- Patronise us; we are capable of learning it

- Just deal with the here and now; take our future into consideration

- Treat us like we know it all because we don't

- Restrict the services on offer to us to particular postcode areas

- Make the systems so difficult that we just want to give up

- Use legal jargon that we don't understand

- Assume that we have the confidence to speak up for ourselves all the time

- Do things for us; instead, do things with us so that we can learn

- Make us feel like we're a nuisance when we ask for help

- Make us feel that we're always starting again

- Leave us out of the loop; our voices could help the case

Yodit's Story

I came to the UK from Eritrea when I was 16 years old, on my own without any family. I lived in foster care to start with, then I was moved into a shared house.

My Social Worker told me I can apply for housing, so I filled in all the forms and handed them in to Social Services. It wasn't until a year later that they told me they had lost my file — I had missed my place on the waiting list and I didn't even know about it. By that time, all the young people who had applied at the same time as me had moved into their own flats, and I had to start again from square one. When I turned 21 I was told I had to move out and find my own accommodation. My Social Worker sent me to the homeless unit, but the homeless unit rejected me because they said I wasn't a vulnerable person. My Social Worker didn't support me to find somewhere to live; she told me I should go and stay with friends but I didn't have anyone I could turn to. At the moment I am stuck in a temporary hostel. I found out recently that I am entitled to a Leaving Care Grant of £1,300. However, Social Services are refusing to give me the full amount — they say I can only claim £500 because they have to use the rest to cover the costs of rent when I stayed on in my housing after I turned 21. Without the full grant I have no chance of putting down a deposit on private rented accommodation. I never understood the whole system; they moved me from one place to another and I didn't know what was happening to me; it felt like no one ever told me anything. I feel like I can't trust anyone who works for the Local Authority or the Government. They say one thing, then the rules all seem to change. No one ever explained how the system worked and I never knew what to expect. If I'd been given proper information about how it works I could have planned my life around it, but as it is I am stuck.

Our experiences of services • Social Services

Employment

Many of us have to wait years for the Home Office to make a decision about our case. During this time we are living in limbo and it's so very hard to get on with our lives. We have to send away all our papers and documents to the Home Office when we apply for asylum, apply for an extension on our leave to remain, or make an appeal against a decision. When we don't have these documents many employers won't take us on – a letter from our solicitor saying we have permission to work is not considered sufficient proof.

"I keep applying for jobs – and I have been offered most of them. But then I go through the whole process, and then at the last stage they ask to see my passport. When I tell them I don't have it, they say 'sorry, bye, there's the exit' "

Many young people who are seeking asylum and don't have permission to work feel forced to work illegally because they don't have enough income to survive on.

Young refugees are under a great deal of pressure from their families to provide an income, whether the families are in the UK or overseas. We want to work, and are prepared to work hard. However, because refugees do not have the personal and family networks through which young people often find their first jobs, we find it very hard to find work, especially if we don't have experience.

"Every day for six months I took my CV to every shop in Oxford Street, and no one ever called back"

Some communities seem to get trapped in certain kinds of work, for example cleaning in the Latin American communities and factory work amongst the Somalis in North London. When the pressure is on young people can find they have no choice but to leave education to earn money doing this kind of work – it's such a waste of our talents!

Young people tend to find Job Centres unfriendly and unhelpful. It can be very hard to understand and negotiate the red tape:

"I couldn't get a job because I had no National Insurance number, and they wouldn't give me a job without one. And they wouldn't give me my number without a job offer, so it was like a circle; I was stuck."

"When I turned 19 I was taken off Income Support and told to apply for Job Seekers Allowance. The Home Office has all my papers because I am applying for an extension, and the Job Centre did not believe that I had permission to work. For weeks I didn't have any money at all – I had to borrow from friends"

Many of us get such poor advice that we end up failing and going nowhere. We need Connexions staff, college careers advisors and Job Centre staff to recognise our strengths and help us to find and use the many talents we have. We are keen students and workers - we need good advice and opportunities to try things out and find out what's possible.

Our experiences of services • Employment

Alfie's Story

I came here from Kosovo aged 15. I did a course with the Princes Trust and did a work placement at an HE College; I did really well there and they gave me a temporary administration job. I ended up working there for 4 years. I had independence, was supporting myself, and learning new skills.

In May 2006 my refugee status ran out and I had to apply for an extension. I had to send off all my papers and documents to the Home Office; the Home Office has now been processing my application for nearly 2 years and I am still waiting for the decision. Imagine how it feels – I've spent a third of my life waiting.

In the meantime a permanent position came up at my work and I was asked to apply for it. I did and I got offered the post – but then they wanted to see proof of my permission to work. I showed them the documents I had, including a letter from my solicitor saying I had permission to work, but they would not accept that – they needed a letter from the Home Office. I telephoned and wrote to the Home Office to request a letter but they didn't respond. Eventually Ros at RefugeeYouth contacted the Director for Borders and Immigration about my case and I finally got the letter – but by then it was too late. The college had offered my job to somebody else and now I am unemployed.

Our experiences of services • Employment

Housing

Many of us have often felt that we are treated without respect or support by Housing Departments. When you have no family or community support networks here, you are totally dependent on the Local Authority for housing, and it is such an important part of life.

"Your home is everything, and you plan everything around your house"

Many hostels are inappropriate for young people as they are often dirty, dangerous and depressing:

"I live in a hostel with 24 others. Everyone who is living there wants to leave"

"There are lots of different behaviours there – everyone fighting, sometimes with knives. I don't feel safe."

"My Social Worker went to my hostel and she was shocked. It wasn't safe; people living there have lots of issues"

Shared housing can be difficult and overcrowded, and big families may be forced to share small houses. Being moved around London can be very disruptive:

"I was in Redbridge when I first came but got moved to Lewisham when I was 16. At 18 I got moved back to Redbridge - even though I was half way through my course in Lewisham. I lost all my contacts and friends"

"Constantly being moved to new temporary housing means you can't settle, can't invest in a place even if it's bad, because you may move out tomorrow"

Our experiences of services • Housing

Some of who arrive here without family are placed with foster families who look after us until we are able to live independently. There can sometimes be clashes and difficulties;

"My foster mum acted like she was doing me a favour and she treated me very different from her own kids. She made me feel like everything she spent on me was coming from her own pocket, and sometimes I felt like she was doing it just for the money"

On the other hand, when it works well, it can really help us to settle here;

"My foster mum really looked after me, told me all the tips of how to get about and stay safe in London. She made me feel like I was her son and even now I go back there in the holidays"

Bam's Story

I came to the UK on my own when I was 16.
At first I was in a shared house, then, when I turned 18 they moved me into my own temporary flat. Ever since I moved there the heating didn't work, and then the hot water broke down.
I contacted Social Services and they told me to contact the landlord. He is very hard to get hold of and didn't seem interested to help.
Social Services told me that they are not allowed to contact the landlord directly because he works through an agency; so they can't make him fix it, and I am left in between. This winter I have been left for 4 months without heating or hot water. Eventually I found out about Voice, which is an advocacy service, and they put pressure on Social Services to do something about the problem.
They have now found me a new place, but the problem is, they won't let me view it – they say I have to decide to move or not move, but I can't see it first – but how do I know that it's not worse than the place I am in now?

If we make it to University, we have to make the difficult choice between coming out of the housing system and moving into halls, or staying in our housing and missing out on University life.

"At the moment I am in halls at my university. It's difficult because people leave on the weekends and the holidays to go home, For me, that is home... but it's like a hospital you know?"

Panzon's Story

I had my indefinite leave to remain, but I was going through a difficult time. I lost contact with my family and I ended up becoming homeless.
In the process I lost my bag which contained all my papers including my travel document, which was my only proof of my immigration status. I needed support to get my life back on track, but without my papers I couldn't access anything. I found that the Job Centre, Housing Office, and even independent housing organisations were not willing to help me until I had proof of my status. I had just started a new job, but they would not pay me my first wages because I had nothing to show them to prove my right to work in the UK. I found it a nightmare trying to contact the Home Office, and when I did get through they told me I had to pay to get new papers issued; but I had no job, no home and no access to benefits – it was like a vicious circle. I couldn't get one without the others. Luckily, through RefugeeYouth, we had contact with someone at the Home Office who had come to visit us. She was able to contact my case owner and he sent the original copy of my travel document. Without that contact I don't know what I would have done. It showed me how difficult it is, if you drop outside the system and you don't have papers, its pretty much impossible to get your life back again.

Our experiences of services • Housing

Health

We have discovered that a whole range of things affect our physical and mental health as young refugees in London.

It can be hard for us to live a healthy life-style. Living on a very low income results in eating cheap and unhealthy food like chicken and chips. Learning to cook for ourselves, often with unfamiliar foods, is also difficult, particularly if we are without our family. Sometimes we don't have access to cooking facilities, or our hostel facilities are so unhygienic that we prefer not to cook at all.

Being moved around a lot can also be disturbing to our health. Since we have no power or control over those decisions, it is a paradox: we move around a lot but at the same time we are stuck. What is more, accessing a GP can be difficult without a fixed address. Not having money to pay for transport also stops us from going to the doctor.

If we go to the doctor, communication can be a problem. It is hard to explain how we feel in another language. We may not understand the doctor or their directions. Without a network of people, it can be hard to find a translator. Some of us prefer not to visit our GP:

"Literally, within ten years in England this is my second time I've been to the doctors. Ten years twice"

"My case had been refused and I was waiting to put in a fresh asylum claim. I needed to visit the doctor, but I can't so I had to go to A&E and just pray they didn't ask me about my status"

Some of us suffer in silence, at times in really bad and unhealthy conditions, as we go through problems with our health and understanding how the system works.

Whilst it can be difficult to access physical health care, it is the mental health issues that we find hardest to deal with, or even to talk about. Many young refugees experience mental health problems because of the traumatic experiences we go through back home, and also because of the systems we go through here.

Coming to the UK alone or not having strong, positive social networks can lead to severe depression. Often we do not know what is happening to us or where to go for help, which makes it even scarier.

"When you come to the country and you are really young, you don't think that you need that mental support, because you don't know what it is, you take it for granted. Smiles become very important"

Many of us come from cultures where mental health is not recognised. Getting professional help for mental health problems can be stigmatising.

"Back home 'depression' doesn't exist, 'stress' doesn't exist. When you act that way, they call you 'white man.' It's not easy to go to counselling"

The pressure of going through the asylum process can also be very negative for our mental wellbeing. We suffer stress and anxiety because of so many uncertainties.

"If you have already gone through traumatic experiences in your own country, living in uncertainty and having people not believing what you are saying has a big impact on you"

Our experiences of services • Health

People see us as different because of the way we speak or because of our background, which makes it hard for us to get on with others sometimes. Trying to 'fit in' to a new culture can make us more vulnerable to unhealthy practices such as drinking, drugs and unprotected sex, especially if we have no one to orientate us on what is right or wrong, healthy or unhealthy.

Sexual health is also a big issue. Many of us have not had sex education in our countries, and so our knowledge is limited. Getting information can be problematic because of the taboo surrounding sex in many communities.

"In our community you NEVER talk about sex; young people are doing it, but they never talk about it"

"In my area there is a sexual health clinic right next door to a Somali Community organisation. Young people are afraid to go in there because they might get seen, and then before they know it, the whole community will be talking about them"

On the other hand, we have discovered many things that we can do to stay healthy, both mentally and physically. Going to the countryside and breathing fresh air makes us feel healthy and free when we have the opportunity. We also enjoy free activities and events in London when they are easy to find and access. Having good relationships with other people helps us to stay healthy too.

"We need to have connections with people here who will support us, introduce us to other places, give us advice and information about the services available to us and so on"

Our experiences of services • Health

Being close to people familiar with our culture helps us get the food we enjoy and to keep some of our cultural practices and celebrations.

Having a clean and safe house gives us peace of mind to rest and sleep, and a private place where we can keep our documents and valuables.

Some of us feel that music and the arts can have healing elements. They make us happy when we need it. Reading, learning and studying keeps us informed of our context and our situation, gives us focus, keeps us busy, and makes us feel useful while we're waiting. These things also give us hope for a better future either here or abroad.

Having our documents makes a huge difference because they give us freedom. While we don't have them we feel like we are stuck in a box, going through endless difficulties, including working illegally under unhealthy conditions.

"Having papers makes things much easier, and the doors open, you can do so many things! It opens up new options"

experiences of services • Health

43

Safety And Crime

Young refugees feel unsafe on the street:

"In my country if someone falls in the street everyone goes to help; here they just walk past"

"Sometimes I find London shifty. There are drunks or bullying kids around, and no one will help me if something happened"

Views about the police are mixed. Some of us feel that they are friendly but that they don't do much.

"In this country people are not scared of the police because they are too friendly, so no one takes any notice of them"

Some of us think the Police target young people who look different, and that we are often stopped and searched for no reason, which is really humiliating.

"I'm not so free because they (the police) are going to pick on me because I'm not from here"

"I get stopped twice every week... It's that bad. I know the people who should be stopped and searched, but they stop me instead"

Many of us have had experiences where we feel we have been disrespected or mistreated by the police:

"I was walking down the street past a group of police officers, and I heard one of them say 'f***ing Somali' about me. I went to another police officer to complain and he told me 'it's not my problem'. They make you think you're mad!"

It can be very easy for young refugees to fall into negative, and even criminal, activity. For those of us who have not been in the country for long, we are looking for a place to belong. We sometimes do whatever it takes to fit in. We often hang around in groups for protection. We sometimes feel that we have to fight to gain respect, or just to survive.

"When I was in school, no one could call me a refugee. I'd fight them because in the back on my mind it was a dirty thing. I didn't know what it meant"

For those of us who have been here longer, we can find it hard to get away from the negative youth culture on the streets.

"I feel like I can't hang around in my local neighbourhood because I will have to join one gang or another otherwise I'll get beaten up by everyone"

Lucy's Story

Recently, World Remix, our weekly youth group went on an outing to see a friend perform in a gospel choir in South London. We all arranged to meet at the station, but two of the young men arrived late so we went on without them (sending them a text telling them to let us know when they arrive).

Just as the concert started I had a phone call from them asking me to come down the road to the station as quick as I can. I went to meet them, and found them surrounded by a riot van full of policemen. The young men had been separated from each other and pinned against the wall. When I asked what had happened, the policeman told me that they had noticed the young men acting suspiciously.

When I asked what they had been doing he told me they had been standing on the street corner looking shifty.

I asked if we could go to our concert, but the policeman said they had to check the identities of the young men first.

The young men were questioned about why they were in Lewisham when they live in Westminster, and then one of the policemen took me aside to inform me (warn me?) that one of them was an 'asylum seeker.' The whole thing took place on a busy high street in broad day light and was so humiliating for the young men who were treated with such disrespect and ungrounded suspicion.

Youth Services

We are keen to find spaces where we can meet friends, socialise, have new experiences and learn, but we often find that this is not what youth services offer. Those of us who have tried to use local youth centres have found them very intimidating unwelcoming places, centred around one kind of youth culture.

"I used to go to a youth club but it was boring. Very white British. I felt excluded because I had no money so couldn't join in activities"

Often there is very little going on within youth centres; just pool and table tennis, football and perhaps a Play Station. Activities can be very male dominated, and there seems to be a real lack of creativity.

"At my local youth centre, it's a great building, but there's no money for activities for the young people"

"Often football is the only option. In the UK it's the main thing and closes out other sports"

Some of us have had some good experiences of creative projects, but they always seem to be short-term. We get involved and then the project ends – there is no continuity. We need to build long term relationships and engage with ongoing activities if we are going to establish our lives here.

Our experience is that many Youth Workers seem to be expected to just supervise and discipline young people, rather than working in participative and inclusive ways which stimulate and inspire young people.

"Some of the Youth Workers just stand there and get paid!"

Our experiences of services • Youth Services

Youth Services are usually divided very strictly into boroughs or postcode areas; if you don't live in the right postcode you can't access what is available. This doesn't work for young refugees; we get moved all over London; we are often living in one borough, supported by social services in another, studying in another.

"It's funny, there are all these problems with young people from different postcodes fighting about 'ends', but the youth services divide us depending on where we come from even more; it doesn't help – it makes the problems worse"

We have also found that youth centres are often closed during weekends and school holidays; the very times when young people need them most. In fact, sometimes we have turned up to access projects that have been advertised, only to find that they don't exist.

Many of us are keen to access the spaces and resources that youth services have; we have a lot of creative ideas about how they could be used, and we have the energy and skills to do the work ourselves. We really believe that youth services should use their resources more creatively, to support independent youth-led projects.

Our experiences of services • Youth Services

Ilhan's Story

We got involved in RefugeeYouth 2 years ago, and it inspired us to go out and make something happen for young people in our local area. Living in an area where a lot of young people were getting into crime we strongly felt something had to be done to support these young people into positive engagement with their community.

The Youth Service made it hard for young people to do something positive for themselves. They made us struggle with their politics and power even though we were all doing the project on a voluntary basis and we did not ask for much except for the use of an empty youth centre. We put life and soul into the empty youth centre but nobody really wanted to recognise what we where doing. The beauty of the project is that it was being run by young people for young people but we felt the more support we received from the Youth Service, the more they wanted to take control of our project, just because we were reaching the young people in the area they could not engage with. The Youth Service nearly made us come to tears at times. Some of the youth workers would refuse to open the youth centre even if there was a large number of young people expecting the project to be running. On one occasion a member of staff refused to let us in the youth centre until the person he was going to hand the keys to arrived, so he made us stand outside the centre to wait in thepouring rain with bags of shopping. We just stood there in disbelief; we felt like we weren't being treated like humans. We felt really pushed out becausewe did not fit ourselves and the project into the youth service's work. Going through this it made us realise young people do not really have a lot of support from the Youth Services and nobody really wants to engage, befriend andcreate positive relationships with young people. Young people are in the media with a very negative image in society today and lots of money is being spent aiming to help young people, but how does it help a young person to leave them in a youth centre to engage with a pool table?! RefugeeYouth, and a Connexions worker who was on our side, helped to put our dreams into realty. Without their support and motivation we would have given up on this project because nobody else truly believed in us.

our experiences of services • Youth Services

Some of our ideas about good practice in Youth Work

What we know doesn't work...

- When adults decide the agenda, be it cultural, religious or moral – they decide what is good for us and push it on us
- Projects that young people see as irrelevant to their lives
- Bog standard youth clubs based on football, pool and table tennis
- Projects based on tokenistic consultation rather than full participation
- When the assumption is that young people cannot be trusted
- When adults create projects around homework, mother tongue or cultural norms, without recognising that young people need social lives too
- Bringing young people together in really forced structured ways for a few weeks, and then nothing
- Services which treat us as numbers, not people

What we think works...

- Projects that support our aspirations and help us to believe in ourselves
- Recognising that 'integration' and 'community cohesion' only happen when people are given real authentic opportunities to build relationships, over time
- Projects that give us new and different experiences; options, variety, lots of arts, non-competitive activities, getting us around London and spending time together on residentials
- When young people are supported to define their own agendas, so that projects are based on what they want and need
- When young people are involved in planning and leading their own projects, so that there is real participation and trust
- Fun, sharing, love, belonging; all the human sides of things that are our most important basic needs
- Projects that are inclusive in a culturally sensitive way

3

Our own solutions

The RefugeeYouth network

Young people from all over the world make up RefugeeYouth, and the network is expanding all the time. Within this network we get inspiration and motivation from each other and have new experiences together; we learn about what is available to us in London and how to gain access to these things; we develop networks of helpful agencies and professionals; we learn practical skills to go out and get active as young leaders within our own communities.

For us, RefugeeYouth is a home, a family, and a place of love and belonging. Our involvement in RefugeeYouth alleviates isolation and stress, and supports us in many aspects of our lives. Through RefugeeYouth we make good relationships with young people from other cultures and backgrounds and other parts of London – we gain a greater understanding of the world in which we are living. Being part of an organisation that asks us to get involved in making the world a better place makes a big difference to our lives and makes us feel good about ourselves:

"RefugeeYouth is a place to be; a place of world peace and harmony; a place for young refugees to not be alone, but feel comfort and patience, gain hope and aspire to be a human being"

"It's a place where our beliefs are respected, where we get help and where we feel the need to give. Here we can discover our creativeness, get stimulation and learning, get access – there are no barriers. Here we can be different, with freedom from categories and constraints, and we can gain acceptance and support"

What we do

In RefugeeYouth we run a whole range of different projects at any time: weekly youth groups, arts events, summer programmes, advocacy projects, and research projects. All of these projects are opportunities for young people to take the lead. We have tried to identify what are some of the ingredients that make our projects work…

The Arts...

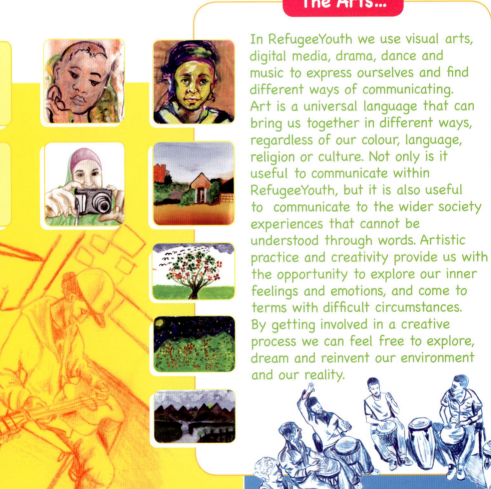

In RefugeeYouth we use visual arts, digital media, drama, dance and music to express ourselves and find different ways of communicating. Art is a universal language that can bring us together in different ways, regardless of our colour, language, religion or culture. Not only is it useful to communicate within RefugeeYouth, but it is also useful to communicate to the wider society experiences that cannot be understood through words. Artistic practice and creativity provide us with the opportunity to explore our inner feelings and emotions, and come to terms with difficult circumstances. By getting involved in a creative process we can feel free to explore, dream and reinvent our environment and our reality.

Residentials...

Going away together as a group on residentials is a crucial and important part of the work in RefugeeYouth. On residentials we share and learn from each others' experiences, and explore and celebrate our diverse cultures. We have found that a residential is essential if we want to do intensive planning and evaluation work, team building and training. This also gives us the option to leave our busy lives in the city, as many of us do not have other opportunities to discover the beautiful landscape of the UK. We use this time to cook, eat and share stories, songs and games in order to build really strong and genuine relationships which can last a life time. Games and outdoor activities give us the opportunity to express ourselves without the need of using words. Finally, through the process of going away together we motivate and inspire each other, and recognise our ability to make changes within ourselves as well as in our peers.

Youth leadership teams...

All young people in RefugeeYouth have the opportunity to take on various responsibilities and leadership roles within the different projects. We take on intensive roles by forming 'core teams' to plan, research, network, make decisions and coordinate activities and events. Some of us are able to take this knowledge back into our own communities and develop and lead projects that bring change locally. At RefugeeYouth, we are supported at all times, and trusted to do the work ourselves. We get training to develop the skills we need in areas like youth work, child protection and first aid. In the past, teams of young people have worked together to create arts events, run weekly youth groups, carry out action research projects, run workshops for students and professionals, and, of course, write this book!

Space

Having our own space is so important to the work we do. RefugeeYouth is a house, a home, an office; we use it as a meeting point, a learning space, a cafe, an art studio, and a media suite. We can also access important resources like internet, telephone, camping equipment, musical instruments. We share the cooking, the cleaning, answering the phone and we plan together how to use the space in different ways. At RefugeeYouth the doors are always open, and we welcome new people into our space everyday. We can socialise, meet friends, feel safe and warm and eat good healthy food.

Mixing It Up...

In RefugeeYouth, we believe in 'Mixing It Up', taking every opportunity to bring together different people to try different things and have new experiences. Our regular 'Mix it Up' arts events are examples of this philosophy in practice. 'Mix It Up' events are planned for and organised by us, as young people, twice a year, bringing together people, workshops, activities, ideas, to create one big, fun day. Usually there are over 150 of us from all over London! Workshops give us the opportunity to learn new skills or develop the skills we already have, like T-shirt printing, DJ-ing, dancing, rapping, art, face-painting, costume-making, drumming and many others. We get the chance to show off what we have learnt in these workshops by performing for each other. After an afternoon of learning new stuff with lots of exciting activities and fun, we eat and party for the rest of the evening.

Why what we do is so important

Supporting Youth Leadership

Despite the many barriers in our lives, young people in refugee communities across London are making hugely valuable and positive contributions to the community, taking initiatives which improve our own lives, and the lives of our peers.

Many of us are involved in running groups, projects and activities within our own communities. We do this on an entirely voluntary basis. We don't expect everything to be done for us; in fact, we have discovered that we can do so much for ourselves, with the right amount of support and recognition, and when the barriers that block us are removed.

Those of us who lead these groups really do know what it means to grow up in two cultures; those of our families and those of the host society. We've experienced it and negotiated it ourselves. We are well placed to lead projects within a strong cultural context, for young people dealing with personal problems such as trauma, isolation, grief, low self-esteem or depression.

It is important to recognise that youth groups of young refugees are different from mainstream youth clubs. The main difference is that refugee youth groups are networks of young people that are active at all times and not just when youth workers are working.

In our youth-led groups, young refugees have become their own youth workers. But we need support to take these leadership roles. We are on a steep learning curve, needing to develop networks and knowledge in London; learning what's possible here and how to get access to the multitude of resources that's available to Londoners; and learning the skills to manage these projects.

There is lots of funding these days aimed at youth-led projects, but so much of it is inaccessible to us because of restrictions and bureaucracy.

Funding for young people:

What works

- Funding that doesn't exclude young people because of where they live, their age, their ethnicity or their immigration status
- Funding that comes quickly whilst our ideas are still fresh and alive; it doesn't work if we have an ambition then we have to wait 6 months for the funding
- Funding that lets us take risks and learn from our mistakes
- Funding that doesn't ask for too many predefined outputs; young people are not very predictable, and if you want us to take a lead expect things to move and change!
- Funding that allows us to measure our own success in our own ways
- Funding that is given to young people to manage themselves – that way we learn
- Simple application forms and monitoring requirements; too much paperwork demotivates us and wastes the time and the energy that we need to spend doing the work

Creating a sense of belonging

All young people need to belong. Young people living in exile leave everything behind when they are forced to leave their countries, including their family, peer and community support networks. Sometimes the only chance to belong is to be found on the street:

"Before I joined World Remix I had some friends from my country. We used to hang about and do things. I did what they did. Not good stuff either. Then I joined World Remix and I stopped hanging out with them. Seven months later those four friends went to prison for burglary. I know I would have gone with them. It saved my life!"

Our own solutions: Why what we do is so important

56

Our youth groups are places where isolated young people can make friends and get to know people who understand what it's like. It can make a huge difference, be inspirational and sometimes life-saving. Young people are very powerful in supporting each other:

"Being part of this group has made my time in London much better, because even though I'm here without my family I have people here who support and care for me"

"I help my friend who has just arrived; I take him to the job centre, to the council, find him a lawyer and an interpreter, show him around London – how to use the transport, where to go"

Life alone in London as a young refugee can be very depressing and stressful. Asylum Policy can have deep emotional and psychological impacts. We need involvement in positive activities with other young people, and youth groups can have a very positive impact on our mental health.

"With the group I feel like I fit in. I like to stay there forever and never go home; seeing people, talking to them – I feel like it's good"

"If I did not find my youth group, I don't know, I would of maybe lost myself in this country"

Moving Forward

Thank you...

...for reading our book, and we hope that you all will take something from it. We all have the power to change things, and it's easier if we work together. We all need to recognise the damaging effects of current asylum and immigration discourse on young people, and work together to campaign against it. We all need to challenge it within the arenas in which we work.

If you are a young person who wants to run a group or project, or just get involved and find out more, please get in touch; the RefugeeYouth family is growing fast, and there is always room around the dinner table for more!

If you work with young refugees, or if you make decisions that affect our lives, then get in touch... let us help to shape the services you offer to young people. We can offer really creative training work-shops; invite us to explore the issues with you...

If you have resources or can help us to access resources then let us know! We are always on the look out for venues in London and in the countryside, sports facilities, tickets to theatres, music events, festivals, ice rinks, bowling alleys ... we're open to ideas too!